Nomad Press

A division of Nomad Communications

10 9 8 7 6 5 4 3 2 1

This book was manufactured by CGB Printers, North Mankato, Minnesota, United States
September 2019, Job #280802
ISBN Softcover: 978-1-61930-769-8
ISBN Hardcover: 978-1-61930-766-7

Educational Consultant, Marla Conn

Questions regarding the ordering of this book should be addressed to
Nomad Press
2456 Christian St., White River Junction, VT 05001
www.nomadpress.net

Printed in the United States.

SPACE ADVENTURER

Bonnie Dunbar

ASTRONAUT

ANDI DIEHN

Illustrated by Katie Mazeika

QUICK! LOOK! A SATELLITE MOVES **ACROSS THE SKY.**
YOUNG BONNIE AND HER FAMILY WATCH **IT GO BY.**

YEARS LATER, BONNIE REMEMBERS **THE SIGHT**
AND THINKS HER NEXT GOAL MIGHT **BE SPACEFLIGHT.**

"I WANT TO BE AN ASTRONAUT," SHE TELLS **HER FRIENDS.**
SHE WORKS HARD IN SCHOOL, WHICH **NASA RECOMMENDS.**

THE *CHALLENGER* LAUNCHES WITH BONNIE **AND CREW,**
AND THEY SEE THE EARTH FROM SPACE, A SIGHT **FEW PEOPLE DO.**

Bonnie Dunbar looked up
into the night sky.

Her whole family stood outside
on their cattle farm, gazing at the
stars, planets, and the Milky Way.

1

They were looking
for something
new in the sky.

There it is!

Sputnik!

The very first manmade
satellite to orbit the earth
was passing overhead.

Sputnik was proof that humans could travel into space.
Maybe they could travel to the moon.
To other planets. **Even to other solar systems!**

After *Sputnik* flew
across the night sky,
many children around
the world went to
bed and dreamed of
traveling to space.

Bonnie was one of them!

But Bonnie would have
to wait to go to space.

She was still a kid!

Bonnie and her family lived on a
farm. They didn't have electricity
or running water.

Bonnie grew up riding horses, milking cows, branding cattle, and picking asparagus.

She drove a tractor, learned how to use tools, and built her own treehouse.

Bonnie and her family
worked hard.

Bonnie also loved to read.

She read whenever she could.

She read biographies of famous people, stories about scientists, and entire encyclopedias!

She also loved to read science fiction. What if, she wondered.

"What if I could go to space?"

When she went to school, Bonnie remembered watching *Sputnik* cross the night sky years ago.

"I want to build spaceships," she told her teacher.

"Then you should take an algebra class," he answered.

So she did.

When you look at an algebra book, you might see both letters and numbers. Algebra is a kind of math that solves problems.

$$2x + 3 = 15$$
$$-3 \quad -3$$

$$\frac{2x}{2} = \frac{12}{2}$$

$$x = 6$$

Bonnie loved figuring out solutions to math problems.

She loved figuring out solutions to lots of different kinds of problems. She took all the math and science classes at her school.

Bonnie still dreamed of going to space.

After high school,
she sent a letter to NASA.

Bonnie got a letter back telling her she needed to go
to college before she could become an astronaut.

FROM THE DESK OF NASA

Dear Bonnie,
If you want to be
an astronaut, you
need to go to college
and get a degree.
Sincerely,
NASA

Bonnie went to college and
worked extremely hard.
She studied and went
to classes and finally
became an engineer.

She still dreamed of going to space.
She applied again to be an astronaut,
but again, NASA said no.
But Bonnie didn't give up.

She went back to school . . . AGAIN!

And the next time she applied—NASA said yes!

Bonnie was accepted to the NASA training program.

FROM THE DESK OF NASA

Dear Bonnie,
Yes! You can be an astronaut.

Sincerely,
NASA

And because she was so close to making her dream happen, she worked even harder.

Finally, Bonnie rode the space shuttle *Challenger* into space.

22

Bonnie looked out the window and saw Earth,
a beautiful blue-and-white
sphere. And she saw all of
the space surrounding
Earth—waiting to
be explored.

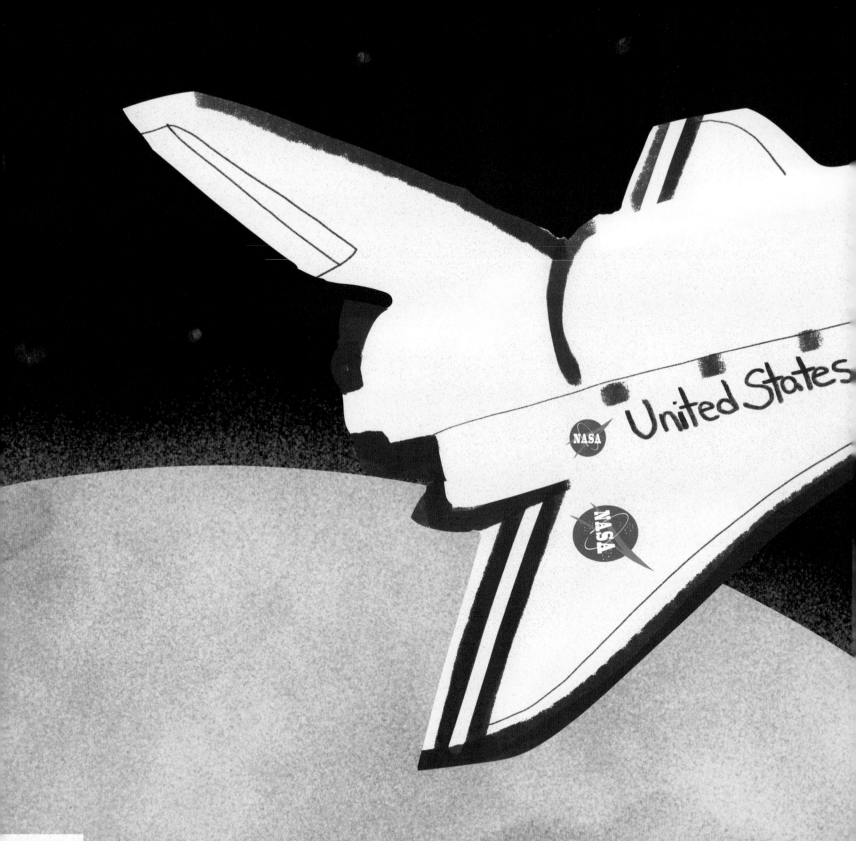

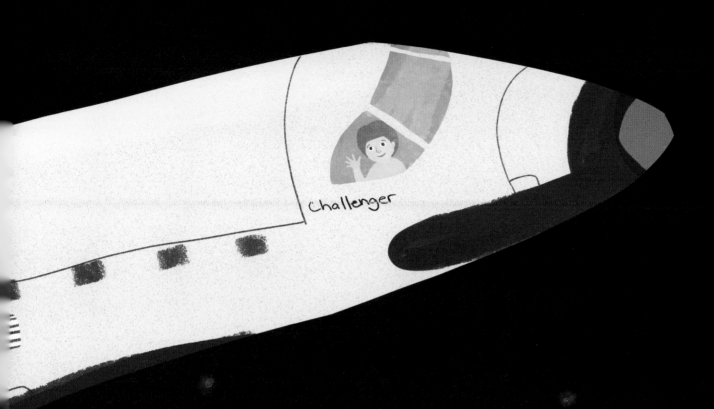

She was the seventh American woman ever to go into space.

After that first trip, Bonnie went back to space four more times. She has spent 1,208 hours, or 50 days, in space. She has flown more than 20 million miles.

That's a long way from watching *Sputnik* pass over her family's farm.

Hello, Extraterrestrial!

Is there life on other planets? Nobody knows yet! But it's fun to imagine meeting extraterrestrial life from another world.

What You Need: paper and pencil, crayons or markers

Do some thinking about what a creature from another planet might look like.

Will they have legs? Arms? A head? How will they get around? How do they breathe? What do they eat? Their appearance will depend on what the conditions are like on their planet.

Draw your extraterrestrial.

What color might they be? Do they need to have scaly skin like a lizard or hair like a dog? What kind of weather do they have on their home planet and what does this mean for their body?

Write a story about meeting your extraterrestrial.

How are they different from you? How might you communicate? What can you learn from each other?

QUOTE CONNECTIONS!

Try these text-to-text connections!

Can you match Bonnie's quote
to the moment in the story?

"When you live on a ranch or a farm, **years are measured by seasons**."

"I just don't see obstacles. I see challenges.
I like solving problems."

"The future of the world may well depend upon
our desire to achieve and to explore. Those
are the engines which result in **knowledge** and
the **solutions** to many challenges before us."

"When I went into engineering, **being the only
female was never unusual to me**. I had a lot
of preparation for that in my youth, particularly
with my involvement in the 4-H program."

"**I always believed that I could do anything**
I wanted to as long as I worked for it."

TIMELINE

1949 Bonnie Jeanne Dunbar is born on March 3.

1957 Bonnie sees the Russian satellite *Sputnik* fly overhead from her family's farm.

1967 Bonnie first applies to be an astronaut at NASA and is turned down.

1981 Bonnie is accepted to the astronaut program at NASA.

A replica of *Sputnik*

Bonnie (far right) and her crew!

1985 Bonnie makes her first trip to space aboard the space shuttle *Challenger*.

1990 Bonnie spends 11 days in space and helps work a robotic arm.

TIMELINE

1992 Bonnie goes to space again.

1994–1995 Bonnie travels to Russia for astronaut training.

1995 Bonnie goes to space aboard the space shuttle *Atlantis*.

1998 Bonnie goes to space for the last time.

Bonnie trains in Russia.

2005 Bonnie retires from NASA and goes to work in Seattle, Washington, at the Museum of Flight.

Bonnie has worked with schoolchildren since retiring from NASA.

GLOSSARY

algebra: a type of math that uses letters and other symbols.

astronaut: a person trained for spaceflight.

biography: a true book written about someone's life.

branding: making a mark on an animal.

cattle: a type of large animal raised for meat or milk or to do work, such as cows or oxen.

encyclopedia: a book or set of books that offer information on many different subjects.

engineer: a person who uses science, math, and creativity to design and build things.

extraterrestrial: life from another planet.

Milky Way: the galaxy that contains our solar system.

NASA: National Aeronautics and Space Administration, the U.S. organization in charge of space exploration.

orbit: the path of an object circling another object in space.

retire: to leave a job.

robotic: describes a machine that moves and performs different tasks.

satellite: a manmade robotic object that is placed in orbit.

science fiction: a story about contact with other worlds and imaginary science and technology.

scientist: a person who studies science and asks questions about the natural world, seeking answers based on facts.

solar system: the collection of eight planets and their moons in orbit around the sun.

sphere: round, like a ball.

Sputnik: the world's first satellite, launched by the Soviet Union (now Russia) on October 4, 1957.

technology: the tools, methods, and systems used to solve a problem or do work.